CRAFTS
OF THE MIDDLE AGES™

THE CRAFTS AND CULTURE OF A
MEDIEVAL MONASTERY

Joann Jovinelly and Jason Netelkos

rosen
central™

The Rosen Publishing Group, Inc. New York

For Lilly, my sweet little flower

Published in 2007 by The Rosen Publishing Group, Inc.
29 East 21st Street, New York, NY 10010

Library of Congress Cataloging-in-Publication Data

Jovinelly, Joann.
The crafts and culture of a medieval monastery/Joann Jovinelly and Jason Netelkos.—1st ed.
   p. cm.—(The crafts of the Middle Ages)
Includes index.
ISBN 1-4042-0759-7 (library binding)
1. Handicraft—Europe—History—To 1500—Juvenile literature. 2. Monasteries—Europe—History—Juvenile literature. I. Netelkos, Jason. II. Title. III. Series: Jovinelly, Joann. Crafts and culture of the Middle Ages.
TT55.J673 2007
271.0094'0902—dc22
                                                                                    2005031470

Manufactured in the United States of America

Note to Parents
Some of these projects require tools or materials that can be dangerous if used improperly. Adult supervision will be necessary when projects require the use of a craft knife, an oven, a stovetop, or pins and needles. Before starting any of the projects in this book, you may want to cover your work area with newspaper or plastic. In addition, we recommend using a piece of thick cardboard to protect surfaces while cutting with craft or mat knives. We encourage you to discuss safety with your children and note in advance which projects may require your supervision.

CONTENTS

MEDIEVAL CULTURE

CHRISTIAN MONASTERIES 6
SAINT BENEDICT 7
A HARSH LIFE 8
THE EVOLUTION OF MONASTIC ORDERS 9
THE DECLINE OF MONASTICISM 11

MEDIEVAL CRAFTS

Life in a Monastery 12
Project 1   Monastery Model 14
Faith and Devotion 16
Project 2   Prayer Beads 18
In the Scriptoria 20
Project 3   Illuminated Manuscript 22
Preserving Knowledge 24
Project 4   Bookbinding 26
A Life of Industry 28
Project 5   Beehive 30
A Monk's Diet 32
Project 6   Pretzels 34
Working the Earth 36
Project 7   Herb Garden 38
Caring for the Sick 40
Project 8   Plague Mask 42

TIMELINE 44
GLOSSARY 45
FOR MORE INFORMATION 46
FOR FURTHER READING 46
INDEX 47

Saint Benedict presents the Rule of the New Order to his brethren in this fourteenth-century fresco by Turino di Vanni. The Rule was a guide for living for medieval monks.

The 1,000-year period known as the Middle Ages roughly corresponds to the collapse of the Western Roman Empire at about AD 476 to the beginning of the Renaissance in the fifteenth century. After the fall of Rome, a period of political, social, and economic unrest took place in western Europe, which includes the present-day countries of England, France, Germany, and Italy.

The beginning of the Middle Ages was marked by invasions from "barbarian" tribes, as the Germanic people who had been entering western Europe for years were called. These invaders from the north and east—Goths, Franks, Lombards, Vandals, Angles, and Saxons—began to thrive once the Roman social and political structure had crumbled. As the end of the fifth century neared, these various Germanic peoples had toppled the empire and Rome itself. A few centuries later, Vikings, the fearless and skilled navigators from the north, also plundered present-day Scotland, Ireland, Normandy, and Russia, looting relics from monasteries and churches. Muslim warriors from the Middle East and North Africa also advanced upon western Europe, hoping to gain territory and spread their new religion, Islam, as far as possible.

During the early Middle Ages, when the fighting between these groups peaked, many western Europeans had turned to Roman Catholicism as a unifying force. Christianity had been the official religion of the late Roman Empire and it would become the dominant force of life during the medieval period. Latin, which was the language of the Western Roman Empire and the church, remained in use, though as the centuries passed, only as a language of scholarship and education. During the early Middle Ages, the only leadership that was able to provide any semblance of normality came from church leaders, or bishops. The force of the Church Militant, as it called itself, showed men how to choose Christ over Satan. Some Christians went so far as to give up all of their possessions to serve God. While some men joined the priesthood, others became monks and lived together in communes called monasteries.

Monasteries served important purposes throughout the Middle Ages. Not only were they places of scholarship, but it was the monks who passed along the knowledge of the ancient world. Monks were literate when most of the rest of the population of western Europe was not. (Without the painstaking efforts of these monks, western Europeans would not have become acquainted with classical Greek and Roman writings until centuries later, when Muslims carried translations of them west.) Monasteries were also places where traveling merchants and

This is a map of twelfth-century Europe, at the time of the Crusades. The Crusades were a series of religious wars fought between Christians and Muslims between 1096 and 1291 to recapture the Holy Land.

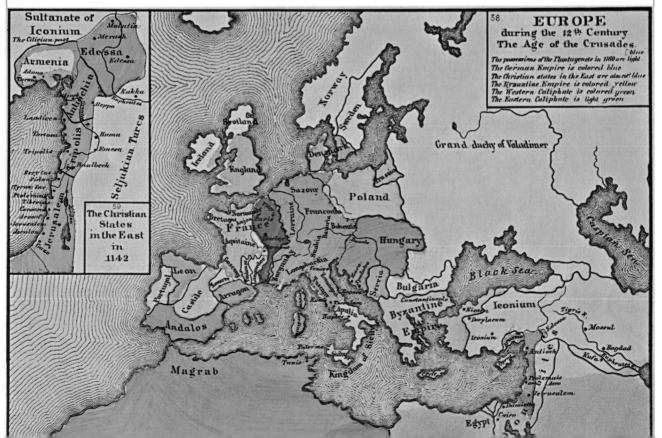

pilgrims could go for a safe night's rest and a warm meal. In many instances, monasteries served the sick during plagues and epidemics. Some monks were expert gardeners and healers. Others were scholars who taught youngsters how to read. While the rest of western Europe struggled through the Dark Ages (as the beginning of the Middle Ages is sometimes referred to because the "light" of the Roman Empire was seen as extinguished), monasteries served as beacons of learning and civility.

CHRISTIAN MONASTERIES

The first Christian monks were travelers into the deserts of Egypt seeking solitary contemplation. Monasticism did not originate from Christianity, however. Certain cultures had practiced monasticism before the time of Christ. Judaism, in particular, had a long tradition of solitary individuals—holy men and prophets—being granted religious insight while wandering alone in the desert. Even so, monasticism is often associated exclusively with Christianity, especially in the West.

Two of the first Christian desert dwellers to win renown were Saint Anthony of Alexandria and Saint Pachomius of Esna. They entered the desert of Upper Egypt to live as hermits in the late third and early fourth centuries. Both had a desire to be closer to God. They felt that the simplest method to find their way was to give up all of their material possessions. This sacrifice helped them concentrate solely on prayer, and it was a demonstration to God of their commitment to him. Their ascetic lifestyle called for them to live in silence.

Soon, entire communities of both men and women had joined the monks in the desert to follow a similar lifestyle. Eventually these hermits were thought of as holy men and women. This form of monasticism is called eremitical, or hermitlike. People traveled into the desert to bring the monks gifts of food and clothing in exchange for advice. Saint Pachomius recognized this movement of people devoting their lives to God and how it differed from the early hermit lifestyle. He then began to organize these communities by developing a set of guidelines for monks, called a rule, especially to discourage all of the charity that had been given to the desert communities. Saint Pachomius wrote that monks living under his rule should not accept charity. He believed they should instead make their own clothing and grow their own food. Under Saint

The monks on this manuscript page are enjoying the outdoors while reading. Monks had a great reverence for nature and spent much time tending to vegetable and herb gardens.

Pachomius's rule, monks were to continue living mostly in silence but could communicate daily during mealtime. Saint Pachomius considered communication between monks to be elemental to religious insight. Although his disciples lived in separate cells, they all worshiped together. This form of monasticism is called cenobitic, or community based. He also urged monks to perform manual labor.

By the beginning of the fifth century, the idea of living together in a religious community had spread to western Europe through the teachings of a Christian monk named Saint Honoratus. People came from far and wide to worship with Honoratus, who eventually established the Abbey of Lérins on an island off the coast of southern France. For more than three centuries, Lérins served as a prominent center of learning.

SAINT BENEDICT

The greatest contributor to Western monasticism, however, was Saint Benedict of Nursia (present-day Norcia), Italy, born around 480. Saint Benedict established rules for Western monks that are still followed today. He was an intellectual yet rather obscure abbot who received his religious education in Rome. Disgusted by political corruption, he fled the city early in life and began a life of solitude in Subiaco, where he lived for three years in a cave. Just as others had worshiped holy men in Egypt years before, Saint Benedict soon attracted a variety of disciples whom he divided in communities. It is with these disciples that Saint Benedict founded a monastery in 529 on a hill in Monte Cassino, about 80 miles (129 kilometers) south of Rome. He chose the site where a Roman temple to Apollo once stood, destroyed its alter, and dedicated it to Saint John the Baptist. The monks who lived in Saint Benedict's Monte Cassino became known as Benedictines.

Saint Benedict established rules for his disciple monks now living with him in Monte Cassino. The Rule of Saint Benedict is noteworthy because it was and is considered the absolute guide for living by all monks in western Europe.

Before the Rule of Saint Benedict was written around 530, all abbots oversaw their monasteries differently. Some were very strict, requiring absolute silence. Others operated more like communes where monks actively engaged in communication and collective worship. The Rule states, "The first grade of humility is obedience without delay." Although God was viewed as the true judge of behavior, monks were sworn to obedience to the abbot, and seven chapters of Benedict's rule describe how to punish monks who disobeyed the rule or abbot. The rule completely exempted abbots from punishment, since any disobedience by them was considered a failure before the eyes of God, who would ultimately judge them after death. Monks, fearing the wrath of eternal hell, listened to their abbots as if they were divine messengers of God.

A HARSH LIFE

By the fifth and sixth centuries, monasteries had emerged throughout western Europe, though it was nearly a century before Saint Benedict's Rule was followed outside of Italy. The Benedictine Rule helped foster a supportive community

This painting of Saint Benedict is part of the collection of the Uffizi Gallery in Florence, Italy. Saint Benedict, though he came from a noble background, left luxury behind to embrace poverty and quiet contemplation.

where monks were expected to work, pray, and study. Each day, they read and copied scripture and other writings. To ensure that these basic guidelines were followed, each day was divided into a careful routine of communal prayer, reading, and manual labor.

A Benedictine monk living in Monte Cassino during the sixth century would be awakened each morning between midnight and 2:00 AM for matins (night prayer), the first of eight daily prayers, which were said with his fellow monks. (The other seven prayers were lauds, prime, terce, sext, none, vespers, and compline.) During Mass, psalms and prayers were spoken or sung, so monks had to learn each by heart. One or two of the seventy-three chapters from the Rule were read during mealtimes, in sequential order, and then repeated again after completion. This repetition reminded the brethren of their duties and service to God. Monks were not permitted to speak during meals, so they developed a sign language to communicate. The remaining hours of the day in between masses were occupied by manual labor such as farming or by tending to fishponds, mills, tanneries, sheep farms, and even stone quarries. (All labor was carried out by the Benedictine monks in their traditional black habits.) Monks also spent their time teaching oblates, or children training to become monks.

Monks were not afforded even the simplest of luxuries. Candles were not permitted. The halls of the monastery were cold and damp, and blankets were only given to the sick. Most of the day was spent in total silence, and monks could not leave the grounds without permission. Even guests were not allowed to visit without formal approval given by the abbot.

Although monks had lives filled with constant demands of service to God, their lifestyle was also desirable to outsiders. Many parents, even from families of nobility, gave their children over to monasteries for protection from the constant war occurring throughout western Europe. Unlike the peasants who resorted to begging for food, monks enjoyed regular meals and an atmosphere of nonviolence. More important, by living as a monk, one was guaranteed salvation for his immortal soul. The life of the soul in the "world to come" was considered of much greater significance than the trials of this earthly existence.

THE EVOLUTION OF MONASTIC ORDERS

Although the Rule of Saint Benedict became the standard by which most monasteries were governed, other monastic orders emerged. It even became possible to choose where one would serve God. For example, a man could choose a monastery that specialized in serving the sick, while another specialized in missionary work, and so on.

By the tenth century, however, some monks feared that they had moved away from the Rule and that their religious lifestyles had become relaxed. Over many years, monasteries had become wealthy, since they received gifts from those who expected the monks to pray for their families. They were also economically successful, self-sufficient communities. Some monasteries had more wealth than nearby churches. Abbots began hiring lay people to work the mills and farms. Monks spent less time performing chores, which were required by the Rule: "Idleness is the enemy of the soul."

In 909, William I formed the Cluniacs, a new order. The Cluniacs wanted monks to return to being disciplined followers of Christ. The abbey of Cluny was immediately placed under the authority of the pope. This period in monastic history is known as the Cluniac Reform, associated with Pope Gregory VII. Unlike the solitary monasteries of Italy, the Cluniac Order was organized so

that all of the monasteries could form a federation under the authority of one abbot. These more unified monasteries were located in villages throughout Europe instead of being isolated. Like the Benedictine Rule before them, monastic federations became widespread.

Another reform order emerged by the eleventh century. Its champion, Saint Bernard of Clairvaux, was also disturbed by the wealth of the monasteries. Saint Bernard formed the order of the Cistercian monks, who returned monasticism to its desert roots of contemplation in service of God. The Cistercian Order grew rapidly, though it would be among the last of the orders that followed traditional monasticism.

At least one monastic order was developed exclusively out of necessity. By the eleventh century, Pope Urban II called on knights to reclaim the Holy Land from Muslims, beginning a series of religious wars called Crusades. In an attempt to liberate the Christian holy lands of the Middle East from Muslim hands, Christian armies were assembled. Over time, more men were needed to fight these wars and protect Christian pilgrims traveling to holy cities. In 1118, a religious order known as Knights of Templar was founded in Jerusalem to assist Christians and fight Muslim armies.

THE DECLINE OF MONASTICISM

Monasteries achieved their greatest accomplishments during the late Middle Ages. Under the collective ownership of the monks, abbots bought inns, barns, and houses in neighboring towns. Some monasteries even controlled stone quarries and ironworks, which were also overseen by abbots. But many bishops thought the monasteries had too much power. Kings even became envious of their enormous wealth. Soon, efforts were made by both church and state officials to control the monasteries.

When literacy began to rise in western Europe, monks were no longer revered as the only educated men. New orders such as the Franciscans and Dominicans provided models for a holy lifestyle that did not demand the same type of financial donations from the populace. Corruption and problems in the papacy resulted in the general population's loss of faith in the church and the monks' ability to help attain salvation. Soon, fewer and fewer monks took vows. As the Middle Ages came to a close, so too did these centers of devotion and scholarship.

The twelfth-century chapter house and other buildings of Rievaulx Abbey can be seen in this bird's-eye view from the roof of its church. Rievaulx was among England's largest Cistercian monasteries during the Middle Ages.

Life in a Monastery

Monasteries or abbeys were some of the most unique residential structures of the Middle Ages. Usually, monasteries were situated on the outskirts of towns so monks could live in isolation. They were often built near streams, which provided water for drinking, washing, and powering mills.

All monasteries contained a church; a garden surrounded on all sides by a cloister, or covered walkway where monks walked; a chapter house, or meeting room; a refectory, or dining room; a dormitory, or sleeping quarters; a scriptorium, or writing room; a "necessarium," or washroom; a library; a kitchen; an infirmary; and a cellar. All monasteries also kept separate residences for their abbots. Larger monasteries had special rooms set aside for conversation, multiple guest rooms for pilgrims and other travelers, and heated rooms for the sick.

During the middle to late Middle Ages, as monasteries grew in both wealth and power, they evolved into

This cloister of the monastery of Santo Domingo de Silos features a colonnade of Romanesque columns. The twisted column was built on purpose as a reminder of the humility and imperfection of man before God.

sophisticated communities that housed farms, mills, fishponds, breweries, cemeteries, stables, and even ironworks. The monks, who worked diligently to support this interconnected network of services, largely benefited from their labors, since they had a constant supply of milk, food, beer, wood, and water.

A series of prayer services shaped each monk's day, beginning with matins and lauds, which were sometimes said aloud with the other monks. After nightly prayers occurred after midnight, monks were again awakened at dawn, which was the start of their day. Before heading to the morning service, or prime, they went together to the lavatory to wash. Next, they gathered in the chapter house for a meeting to discuss matters of the day, followed by reading or studying. The third hour after sunrise was reserved for High Mass and prayers called terce. Sext was said at midday, followed by a midday meal that took place in silence. A short period of recreation was permitted after the meal, followed by none (a short prayer), work in the garden, vespers (a twilight prayer), and compline (a prayer before bed). When work began to distract from these required prayers, some abbots began hiring peasants as laborers.

Educated monks often spent their free time copying religious texts and illuminating manuscripts. Others

Monks gathered in silence for meals in the refectory, where they listened to a reading from the Rule of Saint Benedict. This image is from "Stories of the Life of Saint Dominic," a fourteenth-century manuscript.

appealed to their abbots for time away from the monastery to do missionary work, go on a pilgrimage, or attend a university. Some monks who left the monastery never returned and instead turned to begging in the street to survive.

The twelfth-century monastery of Saint Trophime in Arles, France, showcases typical Romanesque designs of the early medieval period. Romanesque architecture is distinguished by rounded arches and vaulted ceilings.

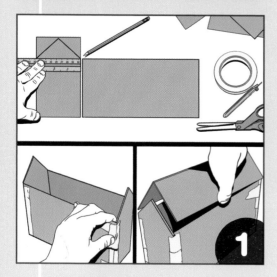

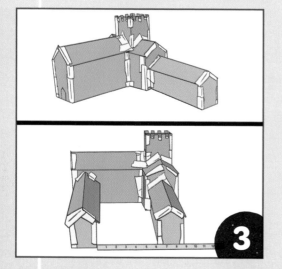

Monastery Model

You can make this model of a monastery by repeating the construction of five similar-sized rectangles.

YOU WILL NEED
- Cardboard
- Ruler and pencil
- Craft knife
- Scissors
- Masking tape
- Brown grocery bags
- Paints and paintbrush
- Glue/water mixture, bowl, brush, and paper strips (for papier-mâché)

Step 1
For the nave (main monastery church), cut two 7x3-inch pieces of cardboard for the front and back walls and three 9x5-inch pieces for the sides and roof. Measure 2 inches from the top of each wall and draw a horizontal line across each, marking the middle. Next, draw vertical lines from those points. Draw lines connecting edges to midpoints to make triangles. Cut away the excess. Tape the sides to the front and back. Fold the remaining board in half, lengthwise, and tape it to the triangular peaks as the nave's roof.

Step 2
To make the transept that crosses the nave, cut from cardboard two 6x4-inch pieces (front and back walls) and three 9x4½-inch pieces (sides and roof). Assemble the structure as you did in Step 1. For the bell tower, cut from cardboard four 4½x3-inch sides and a 3x3-inch roof. Take opposite walls and make a triangular cut out of the center of each so that they fit on the roof, as shown. Tape the sides of the bell tower together and tape it to the roof. Cut ½-inch slits around the perimeter of the top of the bell tower and fold and tape alternate tabs to make crenellations.

Step 3
Make a dormitory that extends from the transept. Cut two 5x2½-inch pieces and three 9x3-inch cardboard pieces. Make another structure that will sit parallel to

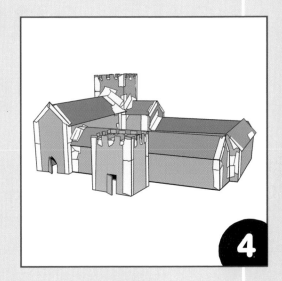

that one out of two 4x2½-inch pieces and three 12x3-inch pieces. Once the two structures are attached with tape, measure the space between them. Make a small building (refectory) to fit snugly in this space.

Step 4
Now make an abbot's lodge by repeating the steps for the bell tower without cutting out the triangles. Cut doorways. Attach the model to a large piece of cardboard.

Step 5
To make cloisters, cut four 7x2-inch pieces of cardboard. Draw a horizontal line ½-inch from the top with vertical lines crossing it at ½-inch points. Connect these lines to form doorways and cut away the excess. Cut four strips of cardboard ½-inch x 7 inches and glue the strips to the bottom of the cloister columns, as shown. Next, tape the columns together in a square. Place the square in the center of the model and cut cardboard pieces to make a roof for each side. Before attaching the cloister and roof pieces, cover the model with papier-mâché by dipping paper strips into the glue/water mixture and smoothing away excess water and bubbles with brush. Once dried, glue the cloisters in place, tape the roofs, and conceal the tape with more papier-mâché.

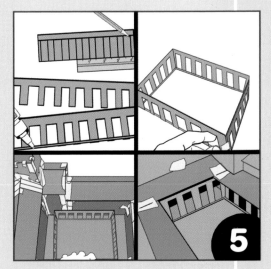

Step 6
Add detail by gluing bits of cardboard in place such as arches. Finish by painting windows, etc.

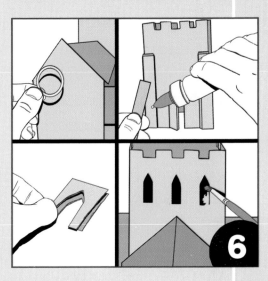

Faith and Devotion

Saint Benedict's Rule was meant to help monks lead a proper life of faith and devotion. To keep monks from living idly, each moment was reserved for prayer, church services, reading, studying and copying religious texts, or manual labor. Many monks also had individual roles within the monastery. A cantor was a monk who presided over singing during church services. A cellarer helped stock the monastery with outside foods and was also aided by a *granatorius*, or keeper of the grain. A monk called a guest-master was in charge of readying the guest housing, and a novice-master kept charge over the novice monks. A monk called a hebdomadarian sang the High Mass each day for one week and was also in charge of giving blessings at church services during that period. Nearly every monk in the monastery had a particular responsibility in addition to his common duties.

A monk's life was certainly one of quiet religious devotion, but it was often

This choir of monks sings from the "Psalter of Stephen of Derby." A psalter is a book of religious psalms or hymns.

lonely. The word "monk" actually comes from the Latin word *monachus*, which means "one who lives alone." Although monks were deeply religious men who found protection in the isolation of the monastery, they very often struggled with depression in silence. Some found solace in routine, while others were comforted by their service to God. Part of that service was the daily recitation of prayers, psalms, and chants, which helped remind the monks of their responsibilities to their abbot and God. Some monks copied prayers and holy passages on wax tablets; others used a paternoster, or

wooden bead rosary to help count prayers said in silence. Up to four hours of each day were reserved for private prayer and contemplation.

Although the term "rosary beads" (wreaths of roses) made its first appearance in print during the Middle Ages, historians know that the origin of beads used to count prayers is actually much older and may well come from India, circa 500 BC. The monks, like other religious devotees before them, believed that the frequency of reciting prayers also made them more effective. For instance, the traveling Knights of Templar, who could not attend regular church services because they were fighting the Crusades, were required to recite the Lord's Prayer no fewer than fifty-seven times per day, a number that was doubled for one week if one of the men had died. To accurately count prayers without a rosary was difficult at best, and strings of beads (each symbolizing one prayer) helped monks record their progress. Even lay people used strung "beads" to help them remember their prayers, but these were usually dried fruit pits, berries, or bones.

A monk strings prayer beads in this illustration from a medieval manuscript. Strings of beads to help monks count and recite prayers were common from about AD 1000.

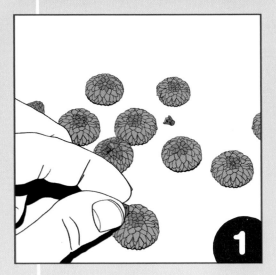

Prayer Beads

Understand the importance of religion and devotion by creating your own prayer beads out of natural materials.

YOU WILL NEED
- Acorn tops (or hollowed nutshells)
- All-purpose craft or wood glue
- Embroidery floss or string
- Cardboard
- Scissors

Step 1
After you have collected your acorn tops or nutshells, examine them. Discard any that are oddly sized or that don't match the others. If you are using acorns, pick off and discard their stems. Cut a long piece of string or embroidery floss in a color of your choice. For this project, we used a 36-inch piece of green embroidery floss and forty-eight acorn tops.

Step 2
Find two acorns or nutshell tops that fit together without leaving much space between them. Bead glue along the edge of one acorn or nutshell. Place the floss in the center of the acorn or nutshell and set another directly on top of it. Press the two tops together, sandwiching the floss or string inside.

Step 3
Tie the glued acorn or nutshell tops together with a small piece of string. (This will help the glue set and will later be removed.) Continue gluing acorn or nutshell halves, approximately 1 inch from each other, until your length of floss or string is covered.

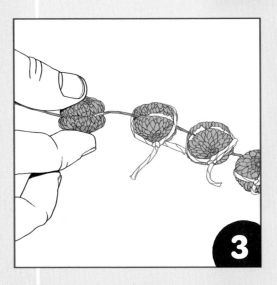

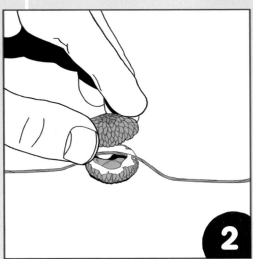

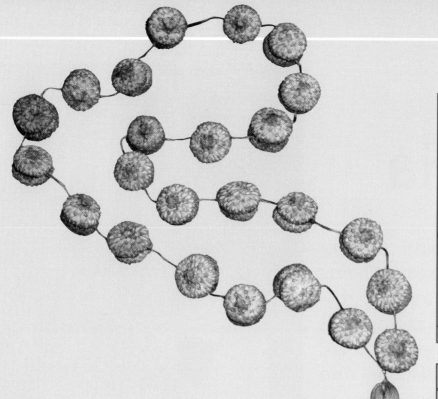

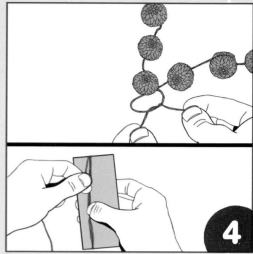

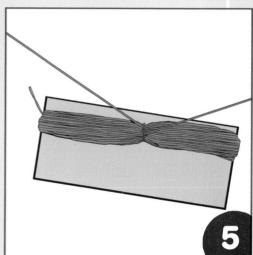

Step 4

Once your strand of acorn or nutshell "beads" is complete, tie the ends together. To make a tassel, take a small piece of cardboard, approximately 5 inches long, and wind a bundle of embroidery floss or string around it, as shown. Since you'll need excess floss, don't cut the bundle away from the entire strand.

Step 5

Once your tassel is as thick as you would like it, lift the wrapped floss away from the cardboard, inserting a short piece of floss under the bundle. Tie it tightly. Remove the floss from the cardboard.

Step 6

Holding the wrapped bundle where the knotted floss is, take the excess floss and wrap it around, about a half inch from the top, making a ball-like shape. Tie the ends of the string tightly. Cut the bottom of the tassel and tie the top to your prayer beads.

In the Scriptoria

A medieval monk sits in a scriptorium patiently copying religious texts. Monks spent a portion of each day copying texts for devotion, education, and private commission for nobility.

From about the fourth century onward, monks worked for hours in their scriptoria, copying religious, scientific, and philosophical texts of the ancient and medieval worlds. The work was tedious and repetitive, but it gave monks time to reflect. This work would be one of the greatest contributions of the Middle Ages. A famous medieval phrase speaks to the level of dedication of the religious scribes: "Two fingers hold the pen, but the whole body toils."

The scriptoria were usually situated directly off the cloisters since the best possible lighting for reading and writing was required. The director of each scriptorium was called an armarius. He gave instructions to each monk and managed the production of all books. All monks specialized in certain aspects of book production. Some were talented artists who created ornate lettering and decorative borders. These monks were called rubricators (named after the red ink called rubrica that was made from red earth) and miniators. Others specialized in accurate and readable penmanship, often working as scribes. The beauty and detail of these early handmade books became the hallmarks of modern book production after the invention of the printing press by Johannes Gutenburg in the 1450s.

Before the parchment could be used as a writing surface, it had to be prepared. Since the first parchment paper was made from the skins of calves, sheep, and goats, it had to be scraped, soaked, and dried before it was written on. Other items required preparation as well, including quill pens that needed frequent sharpening, and the various inks that had to be mixed. (One ink recipe from the Middle Ages required a mixture of three ingredients to be set out in the sun for a number of hours before it would "sooner prove good inke.") Other materials needed included gold and silver leaf that was applied to layers of wet gesso (a mixture of plaster, white lead, water, sugar, and egg whites). Books produced before the invention of the printing press were made of a set number of folded parchment pages that were secured between leather or wooden panels and held together with hinges and hasps (metal fasteners). Some book covers were even encrusted with precious and semiprecious stones, ivory carvings, or enamel.

This enlarged letter D *is decorated with gold leaf. Monks with specific talent for the task often created decorated letters by applying gold leaf to manuscript pages with gesso.*

The plants depicted in the initial letters of this manuscript page were used for medicinal purposes during the Middle Ages. Letters designed with images were called rubrics, and the monks who created them were known as rubricators.

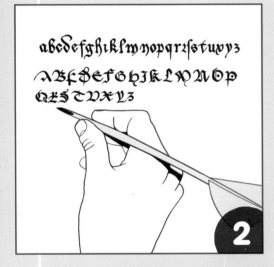

Illuminated Manuscript

Discover the ease and fun of using a quill pen when you write and illustrate pages for Project 4 on pages 26–27.

YOU WILL NEED
- 8½x11-inch pieces of paper
- Craft knife
- Ruler and pencil
- Several goose quills (available at craft/art stores)
- Bottled india ink
- Paints and thin paintbrushes

Step 1

Carefully strip the feathers from your goose quills. Cut the tip of the rooted end in a diagonal with your craft knife. Notice the clear part of the center. This is where the ink will deposit when the quill is dipped in ink.

Step 2

Dip your quill in a bottle of ink and blot the excess ink on a paper towel. Practice writing on scrap paper before you begin your project. Familiarize yourself with the variety of designs that can be achieved with a quill pen, from fine to thick lines. For ideas, examine the manuscript illustrations in this and other books about the Middle Ages.

Step 3

Fold two 8½x11-inch pieces of paper in half horizontally. Cut the pages in half along the fold, making four pieces. Fold those pieces in half again vertically to make a small booklet.

Step 4

Decide what you want to write in your manuscript. You can make your own Book of Hours with prayers and

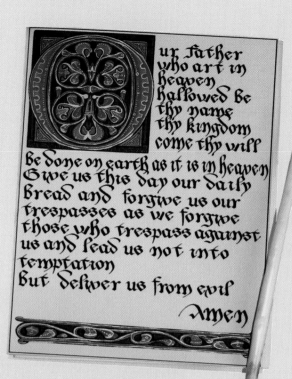

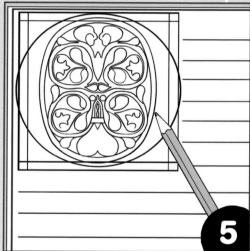

calendar pages marking important holidays, events, and birthdays, as one example. Draw a ¼-inch border around your pages with a ruler and pencil. Inside the margins, draw a square for an illuminated rubric and letter. Next, draw horizontal lines for text, as well as borders for additional illustrations.

Step 5
Draw within the drawn square an outline of the letter that will begin your text. Add designs like scrolls or plants to weave around the letter. Color your letter with watercolors and a fine brush or use your quill and colored inks. Allow time to dry fully between colors.

Step 6
After the ink or paint has dried, outline your design in thin black lines. Use gold paint or metallic ink to gild your design. When your designs are complete and pages are dry, write your text on the page. Continue to fill out the pages of your manuscript as desired before moving on to Project 4.

Preserving Knowledge

Among the most important aspects of monastic life was preserving religious texts and scholarly works from the Greeks and Romans. Without the diligent work of the medieval monks, many classical manuscripts would have been lost to Europe and the West. Monasteries were the only places in all of western Europe that housed such manuscripts, and they were often kept locked in libraries because of their value and rarity.

In rooms called scriptoria, monks laboriously copied scholarly and religious works by hand, which was very time consuming. Some monks would only be able to copy two or three manuscripts per year. There were strict rules regarding the copying of texts. The house rules of the Brethren of the Common Life, an order of fourteenth-century monks from Germany, stated:

...You ought to attend in your copying to things... that you make the letters properly and perfectly, that you copy without error, that you understand the

This is a manuscript page from a fifteenth-century Book of Hours of the Duchess of Burgandy. Books of Hours included prayers that were said during different hours of each day.

sense of what you are copying, and that you concentrate your wandering mind on the task.

Sometimes copied books bore the name of the religious order responsible for the copy. In some cases, the only other evidence as to who made the copy was found on the last page, where he would write notes such as, "Let God increase sense for those who desire to write," or,

"If anyone take away this book let him die the death."

Centuries later, when copying manuscripts became more widespread, learned men called scribes (writers) copied or wrote original works. Copied manuscripts later helped fortify the religious education in monastery schools.

In a few cases, monks earned money for their monasteries by charging a fee to copy a manuscript. Educated men and women, usually of the noble classes, sometimes wanted copies of popular books of the period. These included Books of Hours (personalized books created to divide the day into a cycle of prayers and that included a list of holy days), copies of hymnals and graduals (books of hymns and religious chants), missals (books to help readers follow church services), and Psalters (books of psalms).

This fourteenth-century Book of Hours was created for Queen Jeanne d'Evreux, third wife of King Charles IV of France. Books of Hours were personal books of devotion that were often commissioned for nobility.

Bookbinding

Pretend you are a medieval monk laboring on a commissioned work by binding a book of your illuminated pages from Project 3.

YOU WILL NEED
- Cardboard
- Construction paper
- Printed pages (see page 22–23)
- Paper doilies
- Needle and thread
- Awl
- Glue stick
- Paint
- Paper towel or dry brush
- Ribbon (bookmark)

Step 1
Bind the illuminated manuscript pages from the previous project into a book, or make a blank book. Like in Project 3, take three or four pieces of 8½x11-inch paper and fold them in half. Cut along the folds so you have six to eight half-sheets. Next, fold both groups of pages in half again to make a book. Do the same with a piece of construction paper, making two end pages. Put the pages together with the two pieces of construction paper on the outside.

Step 2
Open the pages and make holes with an awl, about ½ inch apart, along the fold. Puncture through each layer of paper to the end pages. Sew the pages together through the holes.

Step 3
To make the book cover, cut two 4½x6-inch pieces of cardboard. Cut a ½-inch strip of cardboard, 6 inches long for the spine. Glue them to the center of a large piece of construction paper with a glue stick. Fold the excess paper onto the back of the cover. Make diagonal cuts on all corners and a V-shaped cut above and below the spine, as shown. Glue the paper to the inside cover.

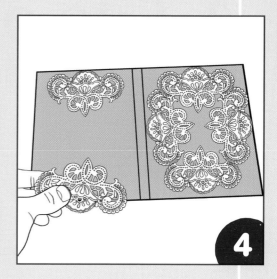

Step 4
To make an ornate design for your book cover, cut shapes from a large paper doily. You can use large and small pieces to create detail. To apply the design, spread a thick layer of paint on the front cover and set the doily pieces into the paint. Next, paint over the doily shapes in the same color. Paint the edges of the cover as well as the construction paper on the reverse side. Allow time to fully dry.

Step 5
After the cover is dry, dab some gold paint onto a paper towel and gently rub the paint onto the book cover. This will bring out the doily design. You can also apply paint using a dry brush technique. For this technique, dip the tips of a dry brush in paint and wipe away the excess before applying. (Do not apply paint with water or a wet brush!)

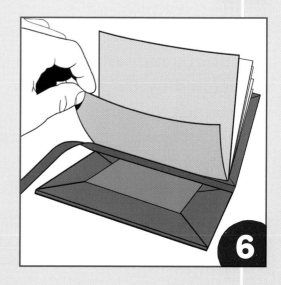

Step 6
After the cover is fully dry, set a 12-inch piece of ribbon inside its cover near the book's spine. Glue the front and back end pages to the inside cover with your glue stick. You have just made a book!

A Life of Industry

In this unusual illuminated Q from a manuscript taken from the Abbey of Citeaux in France, monks are splitting a log. Monks considered manual labor a daily ritual to serve God.

Idleness of any kind was unacceptable for a monk living during the Middle Ages. Life was regimented in order to assure adequate time for prayer, study, and manual labor. According to Saint Benedict, working with one's hands helped a monk remain focused on God and his service to God. According to the Benedictine Rule, monks are "truly monastic when they live by the labor of their hands, as did our Fathers and the Apostles."

There were plenty of jobs to do within a monastery. Most of them were dictated by the seasons. In the winter, grounds were prepared for farming (for the following spring), and fish were preserved in oil, or by salting or smoking. Fruit orchards were pruned in the spring, and by late summer and fall the gardens and farms were ready to be harvested. Other chores were done on a daily basis. Clothing needed to be laundered, food required preparation, gardens needed to be planted and tended to, and animals needed to be fed. These are just a few of the many daily chores that had to be completed in order to run a proper monastery. Assigning these tasks was the responsibility of the abbot. Some monasteries even contained makeshift hospitals and schools that also required the labor of the monks.

Most monasteries produced their own food, which is why most of them either contained fishponds or were built near streams. (For the most part monks were vegetarians, but they were permitted to eat rabbit, which, at the time, was not considered meat.) The monks usually fished daily; made their own beer and wine (water was limited); and harvested honey from beehives. Honey was especially important in the Middle Ages because it was the only sweetener available. Besides its use in cooking, honey was also needed to make mead, a drink consumed on special occasions. Monks obtained eggs from chickens, and milk from cows. They also made butter and cheese. Vegetable and herb gardens provided additional ingredients. Whatever else was needed, such as grain, was sent for by a cellarer.

This beehive was woven in a manner traditional to the Middle Ages. Collecting honey was important during this period since it was the only available sweetener.

Beehive

Try weaving this authentic-looking beehive out of natural materials.

YOU WILL NEED
- Long pine needles (or paper raffia)
- Cardboard
- Glue
- Ruler
- Craft knife
- Twine
- Scissors

Step 1
Cut about twenty-five strips of cardboard, each about ¼ inch wide and 8 inches long. Take two strips and glue them together to make a band. Cut a circle from cardboard to fit the band and glue it around the bottom.

Step 2
Glue the remaining strips along the outside of the band, about ½ inch apart. Pinch the strip in place for a few seconds before moving to the next one. Allow to fully dry. This will be the armature of your beehive.

Step 3
After the glue has dried, gather the strips in sections of three or four and tie them together with string. This will give you more control over the structure while weaving.

Step 4
Weave three pine needles head first through alternate strips. Gently push the needles to the bottom of the strips. Place your fingers between the tied strip

sections to pinch the cardboard, pulling it straight up as you weave. As you weave, keep the space between the groups of tied strips about ½ inch apart. As you weave, the cardboard will become more flexible.

Step 5
Continue weaving until there are about 4 inches of cardboard strips showing. Remove the tied string from the ends. Gather the ends together and pinch closed, making a stem. Loop a long piece of twine around the stem at least ten times and tie it tightly.

Step 6
Take the remaining length of twine and wrap bundles of pine needles around the stem. Cut the top of the needles when completed.

A Monk's Diet

Monks were able to enjoy regular, nutritious meals; sweets; beer; wine; and a variety of fruits, vegetables, breads, and cheeses. Monks were largely vegetarians. Typical meals included vegetables such as turnips, a piece of dark bread, a bowl of grain porridge, some fish, cheese curds, and ale (beer). Although it has been said that monks ate limited quantities in the Middle Ages, new research suggests that many suffered from weight-related illnesses, evidence that at least some were gluttonous.

Monks celebrated some days with feasts and observed others by fasting. At least twelve days per year were set aside for fasting (when no substantial food was to be eaten). On other days, a monk's diet was further restricted. All foods derived from animals, including eggs, milk, and cheese, were prohibited on Mondays, Wednesdays, Fridays, Saturdays, and Sundays. The entire

This detail comes from a fifteenth-century manuscript depicting the lives of St. Mayeul and St. Odilo, two abbots of the monastic order of Cluny. Cluniac monks followed a stricter interpretation of the Benedictine Rule. Here, they are depicted dining in the refectory.

periods of Lent and Advent were also times for food restrictions. These strict guidelines led to some game birds being classified as fish. (Monks who were sick were permitted to eat meat in order to regain their strength.)

Monks worked the farms on specific schedules, with farming beginning in the spring. Because motorized equipment did not yet exist, monks did all of the heavy work by hand, though some used oxen and horses to help pull heavy plows. Crops were rotated from field to field every year in order to keep the earth as fertile as possible. Animals often grazed on fallow fields (fields that were left unplanted in order to preserve their richness). Monks grew barley to brew ale. Orchards were cultivated for fruit. Every monastery had at least one herb and vegetable garden where leeks, onions, garlic, cabbage, and lettuce were grown. Foraging for berries, nuts, and mushrooms was also done during lean times, but this was less common.

Occasionally, during times of religious feasting, special foods were offered as part of the celebration. Religious festivals were held at the height of the Christmas and Easter seasons, calling for traditional recipes. Among those foods featured was pretzels, which some historians believe were eaten during Lent, the Christian period of fasting before Easter.

In this rubric from a fifteenth-century French manuscript, a vintner drains wine from a barrel. Few monks drank water with meals. They mostly enjoyed ale, wine, milk, or mead, a sweet drink made with honey.

A medieval merchant sells pretzels in this illumination from the fifteenth-century chronicle of Ulrich of Richenthal. Pretzels were commonly found at medieval fairs and markets.

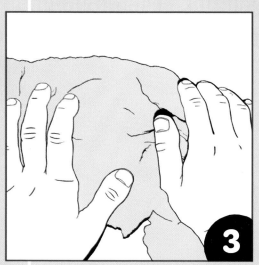

Pretzels

Legends tell us that monks started making pretzels in a twisted shape because they represented hands in prayer. You can make your own flavorful medieval version of the pretzel by following this recipe.

YOU WILL NEED
- Pretzel dough
- 2 mixing bowls
- Spoon
- Dry and liquid measuring cups
- Ungreased baking sheet

Pretzel recipe
3 cups white flour
¼ cup sugar
1 teaspoon cinnamon
½ cup water
1 teaspoon anise extract
3 egg whites

Step 1
Preheat oven to 350 degrees. In a large mixing bowl, combine dry ingredients: flour, sugar, and cinnamon. Mix thoroughly.

Step 2
Separate the eggs into whites and yolks, discarding the yolks, and emptying the whites into a separate bowl. Add and combine with the other wet ingredients: water and anise extract. Mix well and pour into the bowl with the dry ingredients.

Step 3
With clean hands, mix the wet and dry ingredients until you form dough. (Remember to clean your hands and all work surfaces and utensils with hot soapy water after handling raw eggs.)

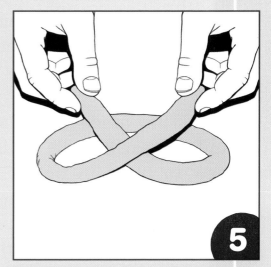

Step 4
Roll pieces of dough on a clean, lightly floured work surface to form a tube, approximately 21 inches long.

Step 5
Bend the dough tube to form pretzel shapes. Wet fingers if dough becomes too dry. This recipe yields about four or five large pretzels.

Step 6
Place the pretzels onto a baking sheet and bake for 25 to 30 minutes or until lightly browned.

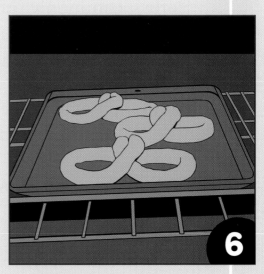

Working the Earth

Medieval monks believed manual labor would quiet a restless soul. Working the fields was exhausting, but it did bring with it a sense of satisfaction, since they believed that providing food and herbs for their brethren was ultimately God's work.

Monks eventually learned to make the most valuable use of their land. They understood how to treat land to make it fertile again. They also knew to plant in tighter densities to crowd out weeds, and some understood how to use animal manure to increase crop yields and to enrich the soil.

Herbs, commonly grown by all monks from the time of Saint Benedict, were especially important to the medieval lifestyle. In fact, Cassiodorus, a contemporary of Saint Benedict, wrote instructions to future monks on their role in providing for the sick. He stated, "I insist that those who treat the health and body of the brethren … learn therefore the nature of herbs, and seek to know how to combine the various kinds for human health…"

In this image, one monk teaches another about specific herbs in a garden. Because monasteries contained the only hospitals in western Europe during the medieval period, passing on knowledge about treatments was considered crucial.

Herbs were in demand by apothecaries, or drug makers, who used them in their potions and ointments. Herbs were also used to enhance the flavor of foods, especially those made salty during the process of preservation. Herbs were often added to ale, milk, vinegar, and honey for home remedies. Herbal remedies were given for wounds like dog bites, as

well as more common ailments, including sunburn and sour stomach. Herbs for medicinal purposes were often grown together in a cloister garden. These included Saint-John's-wort, sage, marjoram (used to treat swelling), mint, lemon balm (used to treat fevers), and dill. Less common herbs included feverfew (used to treat headaches), lungwort (for cough and chest congestion), wormwood (to rid the system of worms), pimpinella, and pennyroyal. There were even routines associated with the proper picking of herbs, which was done in total silence, at daybreak, and often facing south or east.

While it is widely accepted that Europeans understood far less about the human body and its ailments during the Middle Ages than did Muslim societies in the Middle East, there is now evidence to suggest that monks knew more than previously believed about medicine. Monks used hemlock to treat pain, and they also employed regular surgical procedures to successfully amputate limbs, induce birth, and perform simple operations.

The herb calendula is pictured in an illustration from De Materia Medica, *a popular medical manuscript from the fifteenth century.*

Herb Garden

Monks grew herbs for a variety of reasons, including treating the sick. You can grow your own herbs like monks did during the Middle Ages.

YOU WILL NEED
- Herb plant seeds
- Styrofoam cups
- Brown paint
- Paintbrush and paper towels
- Toothpicks
- Scissors and paper
- Masking tape
- Small stones
- Potting soil

Step 1
Write the names of the plant seeds you are going to grow on a piece of paper. Make the titles of your plants approximately 4 inches long. You can also photocopy this page and use these titles by enlarging the image. For this project, we chose herbs that are commonly used in modern cooking, such as basil, sage, thyme, and rosemary, just to name a few.

Step 2
Cut out the titles and tape them to the cups along the outer edges. You can separate long titles by cutting them in half and stacking the words. Carefully outline the letters through the paper, pressing firmly into the Styrofoam with a toothpick.

Step 3
Remove the taped paper and retrace the lines with your toothpick. Press firmly, but use care not to puncture the cups.

Step 4
After your titles are on your cup planters, cover the entire surface with brown paint. Make sure your paint gets into all the crevasses of the etched lines. With a

paper towel, wipe and pat away excess paint. The etched lines will appear darker than the rest of the cup. Let the cup dry before painting about 2 inches of the inside lip and interior cup.

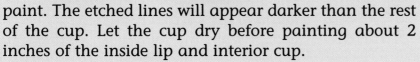

Step 5
Once your planters are completely dry, fill them to about 1 inch from the bottom with small stones. Next, fill the planters with potting soil on top of the stones. Before planting, carefully read the instructions on your seed packets. Plant your seeds according to those directions.

Step 6
After your seeds have been planted, place your medieval herb pots in a sunny window. Water according to seed instructions.

Caring for the Sick

This image of a monk bleeding a patient was found in the Luttrell Psalter, a medical manuscript from the fourteenth century. Monks believed that bleeding a patient would help remove toxins from his or her body.

Although monks were not trained as physicians, many of them cared for laypeople who were either sick or dying, especially during times of great plagues and epidemics. It is now suggested that more than half of all hospitals in medieval Europe were affiliated with monasteries. Most monks could read and write in Latin. They studied all the books they could find on medical topics and many learned a great deal from herbals, books that listed each herb and its medicinal properties and uses.

Their desire for knowledge could not have come at a more appropriate time. In 1347, Europe was hit by waves of bubonic plague, or the black death, which first arrived in Sicily. From that year onward, the plague devastated the population of western Europe, reducing it by more than 30 percent in little more than half a century. Only the coldest climates were spared. One fourteenth-century monk wrote about it from a monastery in England:

It filled the whole world with terror. In places not even a fifth part of the people were left alive. So great an epidemic had never been seen nor heard of before this time, for it is believed that even the waters of the flood which happened in the days of Noah did not carry off so vast a multitude.

40

The majority of people feared that the plague was God's way of judging them. Others believed that the terrible sickness was a mark of the end of the world. Some turned to monasteries for help, but the monks, despite their cleanliness, found themselves just as afflicted by the illness.

Some, out of desperation, requested help from doctors who would keep fragrant herbs to their noses in order to avoid the horrible stench of death and to hopefully avoid breathing in the "vapors" which they thought spread the disease. Besides, Galen, the famous Greco-Roman physician, had written prior to his death in AD 200 that diseases were transmitted from person to person via miasmas, or poisonous aromas. This theory of disease carried into the Middle Ages.

People were advised against remaining in low, swampy areas where it was believed that miasmas could rise up and kill. Many people fled to the colder areas. But physicians wrongly advised people not to wash, believing that doing so "opened the pores," allowing disease to creep in. Most people were told to stay indoors. When people did venture outside, they carried small bouquets of flowers and held them up to their noses to avoid breathing foul air.

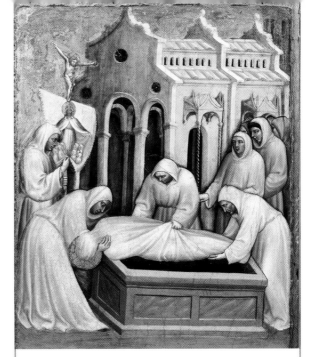

Monks wrap the body of a plague victim in this anonymous painting from the fourteenth century. In many cases, monasteries were the only places where people suffering from epidemics could turn.

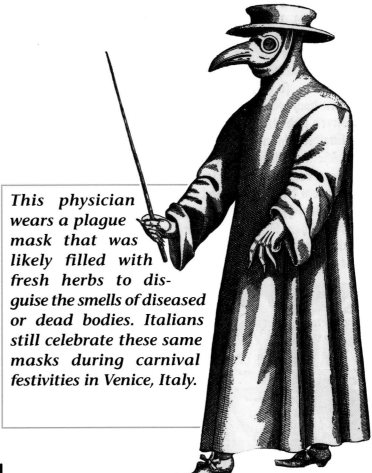

This physician wears a plague mask that was likely filled with fresh herbs to disguise the smells of diseased or dead bodies. Italians still celebrate these same masks during carnival festivities in Venice, Italy.

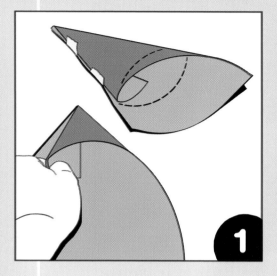

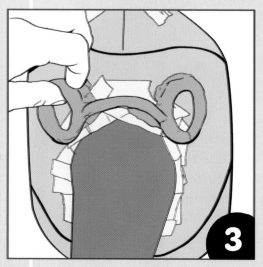

Plague Mask

Relive the frightening epidemic of the black plague by making this "plague" mask, which may have been worn by medieval doctors.

YOU WILL NEED

- Heavy construction paper
- Empty gallon milk jug
- Sand or small rocks
- Masking tape
- Scissors
- Marker
- Modeling clay
- Brown grocery bags
- Paints and paintbrushes
- Awl
- String or elastic cord
- Glue/water mixture, bowl, brush, and paper strips (for papier-mâché)

Step 1

Roll your piece of construction paper to form a cone (the bird beak) and securely tape along the paper's edge to hold it in a cone shape. Cut the excess paper to make the cone an appropriate size for your face. Next, cut ½-inch slits along the wide opening of the cone and fold them back to make tabs.

Step 2

Fill the bottom of the milk jug with sand or small stones to weigh it down while working. Tape the cone to the center of the jug, the opposite side from the handle. Draw the outline for the eyes and mask with a marker.

Step 3

Roll modeling clay to form long tubes, like worms, about 5 inches long. Make the worms into two thin circles for the eyeholes and connect them with additional clay to make them look like glasses. Press the edges of the clay into the milk jug so they stay in place but keep their form.

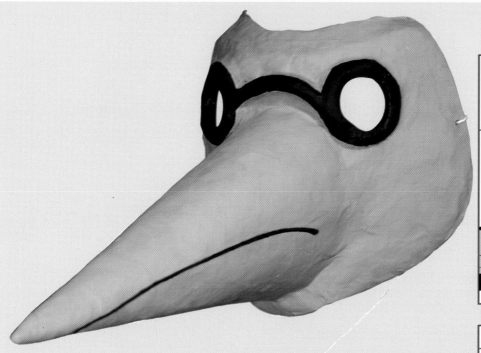

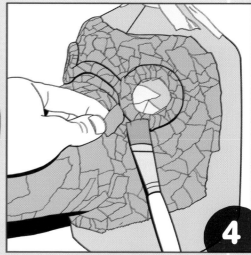

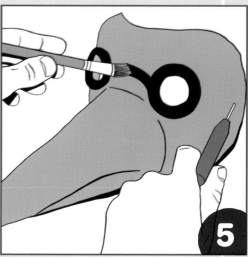

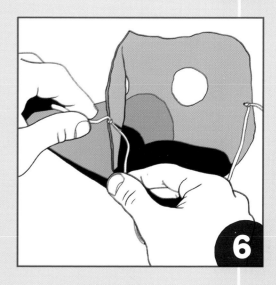

Step 4

Cover the entire surface of the mask with small ripped pieces of paper covered in the glue/water papier-mâché mixture. Smooth away excess water and bubbles with a brush. (Three or four layers of glued papier mâché will make your mask stronger.) After the paper has fully dried, remove the mask from the jug by putting your hands behind the left and right sides and gently pulling. You may have to peel off the masking tape as you remove the mask. Remove any excess clay attached to the backside of the mask, or papier mâché over it with an additional inside layer. Allow additional time to dry.

Step 5

Use scissors to trim the rough edges of the mask, removing any tape from the interior paper cone. Take an awl and carefully puncture holes on the left and right sides. Paint the mask as you wish, allowing time to dry.

Step 6

After the mask has dried, thread a 12-inch piece of string or elastic cord through each hole and tie each in place with knots on the interior side.

TIMELINE

AD | **313** | Constantine imposes the Edict of Milan, preaching tolerance for Christianity.

410 | Visigoths sack Rome.

circa 476 | The Roman Empire falls.

476–1000 | The period historians sometimes refer to as Europe's Dark Ages.

circa 700 | Feudal system is established in France.

711 | Muslims invade Spain.

768 | Charlemagne becomes king of the Franks.

793 | Beginning of Viking raids in England.

1066 | William the Conqueror conquers England.

1095 | Pope Urban II urges Christian knights to defend Christianity.

1096–1291 | The Christian Crusades are launched to recapture the Holy Land from Muslims.

1161 | First guilds are established; the era of cathedral-building begins.

1171 | The Bank of Venice opens.

1179 | The third Lateran Council decrees all cathedrals must have schools.

1180 | Windmills first appear in Europe.

1215 | The fourth Lateran Council requires Jews to wear identifying badges; signing of the Magna Carta.

1241 | Mongols invade Europe.

1271 | Marco Polo travels to Asia.

1300 | Feudalism ends.

1314-1322 | The great famine (alternate droughts and heavy rains in northern Europe).

1337–1453 | Hundred Years' War between England and France.

1347–1530 | The plague kills about 25 million people throughout Europe.

1381 | Peasants' Revolt.

1453 | The fall of Constantinople to Ottoman Turks (often taken as end of Middle Ages).

GLOSSARY

abbot The male leader of a monastery or abbey.

cenobitic Of or related to communal living in a monastery.

Crusades A series of religious wars fought between Christians and Muslims that occurred during the Middle Ages between 1096 and 1291.

Dark Ages An outdated term that is often used to describe the early period of the Middle Ages because of its isolationism and widespread illiteracy.

disciple A religious man who follows the teachings of a monk.

eremitical Of or related to living alone; hermitlike.

habit A long tunic worn by monks.

illuminating The medieval art of decorating a manuscript with colorful ornamentation and figures.

manuscript A document written by hand, taken from the Latin words *manus* (hand) and *scriptus* (written).

matins The first morning prayers—usually at 2:00 AM—for Benedictine monks.

Middle Ages A period in western Europe between the fall of the Roman Empire and the beginning of the Renaissance in 1450.

monk A religious man devoted to living a simple life without any luxuries or outside influences.

novice A man who lived and worshiped in a monastery, but who was not fully considered a monk.

oblate A child given over to a monastery, where he was taught to become a monk.

pilgrimage A journey made by a pilgrim to a religious site or holy city.

plague A deadly disease that was spread by fleas on rats that came into Europe by boat beginning in 1347. The bubonic plague, or black death, killed more than a third of Europe's population in about fifty years.

psalm A religious song or poem, often recited during Mass or other religious services.

scriptorium A room in a castle or monastery where manuscripts were copied by hand in calligraphy.

FOR MORE INFORMATION

The Cloisters
Fort Tryon Park
New York, NY 10040
Web site: http://www.metmuseum.org/

The Metropolitan Museum of Art
1000 Fifth Avenue
New York, NY 10028-0198
(212) 535-7710
Web site: http://www.metmuseum.org/

WEB SITES

Due to the changing nature of Internet links, the Rosen Publishing Group, Inc., has developed an online list of Web sites related to the subject of this book. This site is updated regularly. Please use this link to access the list:

http://www.rosenlinks.com/ccma/memo

FOR FURTHER READING

Anderson, Dale. *Monks and Monasteries in the Middle Ages*. Milwaukee, WI: World Almanac Library, 2005.

Cels, Marc. *Life in a Medieval Monastery*. New York, NY: Crabtree Publishing, 2004.

McAleavy, Tony. *Life in a Medieval Abbey*. Gordonsville, VA: Enchanted Lion Books, 2003.

Sherrow, Victoria. *Life in a Medieval Monastery*. San Diego, CA: Lucent Books, 2001.

INDEX

A

Advent, 32
Anthony, Saint, 6
apothecaries, 36
armarius, 20

B

Benedict, Saint, 7–8, 28, 36
   rule of, 8–10, 16, 28
Bernard, Saint, 10
Brethren of the Common Life, 24
bubonic plague, 40–41

C

cantor, 16
Cassiodorus, 36
Catholicism, 4
cellarer, 16, 29
children, 9
Christmas, 33
Church Militant, 5
Cistercian Order, 10
Cluniac Order, 10
Crusades, 10, 17

F

fasting, 32, 33
Franciscans, 11

G

Galen, 41
Gutenburg, Johannes, 20

H

hebdomadarian, 16
hermit, 6
Honoratus, Saint, 7

J

Judaism, 6

K

Knights of Templar, 10, 17

L

Latin, 4–5, 40
Lent, 32
Lérins, 7

M

medicine and herbs, 36–37, 41
monasteries
   pre-Christian, 6
   purposes of, 5
monasticism
   cenobitic, 7
   decline of, 11
   and depression, 16
   and diet, 29, 32–33
monk, origin of term, 16
Monte Cassino, 8, 9
Muslims/Islam, 4, 5, 10, 37

P

Pachomius, Saint, 6
   rule of, 6–7
paternoster, 16
pope, 10
prayers, daily, 9, 13

R

rubrica, 20

S

scribes, 25
sign language, 9

U

Urban II (pope), 10

ABOUT THE AUTHOR/ILLUSTRATOR

Joann Jovinelly and Jason Netelkos have collaborated on many educational projects for young people. This is their second crafts series encouraging youngsters to learn history through hands-on projects. Their first series, *Crafts of the Ancient World*, was published by the Rosen Publishing Group in 2001. They live in New York City.

PHOTO CREDITS

Cover (center), pp. 12, 21 (bottom), 24, 25 (top), 37 (bottom) © Archivo Iconografico, S.A./Corbis; p. 4 © Arte & Immagini srl/Corbis; p. 5 Courtesy of the University of Texas Libraries, The University of Texas at Austin; pp. 7, 36 HIP/Art Resource, NY; pp. 8, 29 (top), 41 (top) Scala/Art Resource, NY; p. 11 © English Heritage/Topham-HIP/The Image Works; p. 13 (top) © The Art Archive/ Museo di Capodimonte, Naples/Dagli Orti (A); p. 13 (bottom) © Dan Herrick/ Lonely Planet Images; pp. 16, 17 (top) The Art Archive/Bodleian Library Oxford; p. 17 (bottom) Stadbibliothek Nürnberg, Amb. 317.2, f. 13r; p. 20 The Art Archive; p. 21 (top) © The Cleveland Museum of Art 2004; p. 25 (bottom) Metropolitan Museum of Art, The Cloisters Collection, 1954 (54.1.2), Photograph © 1985 The Metropolitan Museum of Art; p. 28 The Art Archive/Bibliothèque Munipale Dijon/Dagli Orti; p. 29 (bottom) Réunion des Musées Nationaux/Art Resource, NY; p. 32 Musee Conde, Chantilly, France/Bridgeman Art Library; p. 33 (top) Centre Historique des Archives Nationales, Paris, France, Lauros/ Giraudon/Bridgeman Art Library; p. 33 (bottom) © Gianni Dagli Orti/Corbis; pp. 37 (top), 40 Erich Lessing/Art Resource, NY; p. 41 (bottom) © Bettmann/ Corbis. All crafts designed by Jason Netelkos and Joann Jovinelly. All craft illustrations by Jason Netelkos. All craft photography by Joann Jovinelly.

Special thanks to Christina Burfield for her continued support and encouragement.

Designer: Evelyn Horovicz; Editor: Leigh Ann Cobb
Photo Researcher: Nicole DiMella